AF365919

Mellow

Regina Adaora Agokei

Mellow © 2022 Regina Adaora Agokei

All rights reserved.

No part of this publication may be reproduced, stored in a retrieval system, or transmitted, in any form or by any means, electronic, mechanical, photocopying, recording or otherwise, without the prior written permission of the presenters.

Regina Adaora Agokei asserts the moral right to be identified as author of this work.

Presentation by *BookLeaf Publishing*

Web: www.bookleafpub.com

E-mail: info@bookleafpub.com

ISBN: 9789357614719

First edition 2022

I dedicate this book to my family, friends, people I have serendipitously met, and to you, the reader. It is you all that make me what I am.

PREFACE

This book is a compilation of poems I have written and re-written at different points in my life. At the time of publication, some were two years old or more, while others, I wrote within twenty-one days in keeping with the Bookleaf challenge. I have always written down lines as they spontaneously came to me, and those lines only emerged as poems after days, weeks and years of letting them sit in my notes, in a process I call "marinating." I always enjoyed a private burst of excitement when lines that had seemed disjointed and unrelated found their way to each other in a combination that just made sense. I am now sharing some of these lines with you, reader, and I hope at least one sparks excitement in you.

Burst

With a heart of peace,
I am
bursting with a world
that I consumed.
It is milky,
it is shimmery,
it is cold,
and I feel myself swell
as it expands within me.

All Things Great And Small

Everything comes from the earth,
everything is connected--
related to the land,
related to the water,
related to the atmosphere--
including all our inventions,
including you and me,
intertwined and coexisting,
made of the same stuff.

Bus Trip

My heart is far away--
broken glass,
a biplane,
measurements for a gate,
dog--
the calm after the storm,
or the stillness before?

One Love

one million sunflowers
ache and bathe
together in the moonlight
after their morning sultry tryst
with the one love
they all share

Union

5

I see a flame,
I see fire,
I see Light,
I see life--
a canvas of union.

Enraptured

Like a hummingbird,
my heart is frantically beating--
senselessly, helplessly enraptured by you,
and I do not know what to do,
and I do not want to let go,
and you will not let me let go.

Need

We are, at once, misery and salvation to each
other.
Your absence and your presence turn me inside
out.
And although I fear how we may ruin each
other,
I am lit with excitement when you say my name.
A warmth expands in my belly,
and all I need is for you
to be here
and be sweet to me.

Patience

I knew you would not stay--
I knew--
but I kept hoping.
And when the time came for you to go
and you left quickly,
I still kept hoping.
And even though I did not know what I was
hoping for,
I kept hoping.
And now,
still,
I am hoping.

Bodies

You are almost not alone when you are next to
another body,
but these bodies are walls,
and these walls cannot be breached,
and these walls do not open for anything.
But how much loneliness can you endure
before you become a twisted thing?
And is there any saving you after that?

Estranged

I only ever wanted
to show you my best
but I was hardly ever that,
so I hid from you,
and I still have not found my way
out of hiding.

Endurance

Bittersweet,
bile green- cotton candy pink.
"What if we die
 to join the clouds
churning in the sky?"
My mind wanders again,
And I must remind myself-
"Keep it together,
don't fall apart,
endure."

Meat

12

Meat, skin, muscle, bone, blood--
the animating force leaves,
and the body which no longer moves
dies and decays.
Meat--
meat for meat,
and meat for soil.

Hunger

Such a hungry thing you are.
Your tongue curls out,
your stomach vibrates,
I stare into the gaping void of your mouth,
and I move to taste your lips.
Will you bite or let me be?
You are a hungry thing--you devour,
and I extend from you
as you absorb me.

Disorder

The great disruptor exists
because everything that is in order
must slowly but surely
descend into disorder-
a new order.

Inheritance

15

Where are they?

They are not here.

Where have they gone?
They are in the ground
beneath your feet.

Where have they gone?
They are in your cells,
they are in the air-
they are Here.

Residue

I want to touch your life
and leave behind my fingerprints,
But I do not need to stay.
Just a hint of me
that you cannot forget is enough.

myself-yourself

I am you
and you are me,
and in this war
we are fighting,
we are fighting
ourself.

Empathy

You do not know
if it is because of the emptiness around you
that your screams fade into nothing
or because you are empty
that you make no sound at all,
but maybe there is
someone else who feels it too.

Age

I seem to be getting
more foolish with age,
and I am in a constant battle
to remember my Self,
but my Self is constantly changing--
shifting--
becoming harder and harder to grasp.

These Things

These things I have found to be sobering:
the way my dust settles on everything;
parting with a precious friend;
the pain I see you are suffering;
a kind of love that does not exist;
this self-made prison.

These things I have found to be amusing:
a blue star-shaped balloon floating through
carefree clouds;
the scintillating voice of a new friend;
your unbridled mirth at a well-placed joke;
the miracle that we met;
that nameless light beckoning outside.

Retrospect

Every new day was a trying hard
to resist the tempting call
of what appeared to be
blissful oblivion,
a trying to grow older
and dreading it all the same.
Eyes looked as they look-
senses taking in all they could,
becoming duller and duller with time.
And in the last moment,
as eyes looked their last,
all the trying seemed
at least worthwhile.

www.ingramcontent.com/pod-product-compliance
Lightning Source LLC
LaVergne TN
LVHW041301200726
843507LV00014B/3075